Who ... Zendaya?

Who Is Zendaya?

by Kirsten Anderson

illustrated by Manuel Gutierrez

Penguin Workshop

To Zendaya—MG

PENGUIN WORKSHOP
An imprint of Penguin Random House LLC, New York

First published in the United States of America by Penguin Workshop,
an imprint of Penguin Random House LLC, New York, 2022

Visit us online at penguinrandomhouse.com.

Library of Congress Cataloging-in-Publication Data is available.

Printed in the United States of America

ISBN 9780593523476 (paperback)   10 9 8 7 6 5 4 3 2 1 WOR
ISBN 9780593523483 (library binding)   10 9 8 7 6 5 4 3 2 1 WOR

Contents

Who Is Zendaya?

On September 20, 2020, Zendaya sat down with her family to watch television. It could have been any ordinary family night. But this night was special.

Zendaya was wearing a glamorous designer gown and full movie-star makeup. Her hair was swept into an updo. It wasn't what she would usually wear just to hang out at home. But she had a good reason to be so fancy. It was the night of the 72nd Emmy Awards. And Zendaya was nominated for Outstanding Lead Actress in a Drama Series for her role on the HBO series *Euphoria*.

The Emmys are given out by the Academy of Television Arts and Sciences. Usually, they are presented in a big theater in Hollywood, with all the stars walking along a red carpet into the event. But in the fall of 2020, the COVID-19 pandemic was still raging. Large indoor gatherings were considered unsafe. So, instead, Emmy nominees got dressed up and watched from their homes. A messenger from the awards show waited outside each nominee's house with the award statue. If the nominee won, the messenger could hand them their trophy. If they lost, the messenger would simply leave.

Zendaya didn't expect to win. The other nominees were much more experienced than she was. Most of them had won other important acting awards during their careers. She felt honored just to be on the same list as them.

Many awards were given out during the show. Winners and presenters made jokes and speeches. Then, finally, it was time for the Outstanding Lead Actress category.

Livestreams began from each nominated

actor's home so the TV audience could watch their reactions in real time. Zendaya sat quietly with her family as the Emmy show host read each nominee's name. Then, he opened the envelope that held the name of the winner and said, "And the Emmy goes to . . . Zendaya, for *Euphoria*."

Zendaya gasped and covered her mouth with her hand. Her family began to scream. She could hardly believe what she had heard. But when her assistant handed her the Emmy Award statue, she knew it was true. And she was expected to say something.

She caught her breath and turned to the camera. "This is pretty crazy!" Zendaya said. She thanked her family and the cast and crew of the show. But then she spoke to her fans.

"I know this feels like a really weird time to be celebrating, but I just want to say that there is hope in the young people out there . . . ," she said. "And I just want to say to all my peers out there doing the work in the streets, I see you, I admire you, I thank you, and yeah, thank you so, so much!"

Zendaya had started out as one of many cute child actors. Now she had become the youngest woman to win one of the most important acting awards in Hollywood. Along the way, she has been a singer, dancer, writer, fashion icon, and a spokesperson for people of color. Most of all, she has always been true to herself.

And it all began with a shy little girl who watched Disney Channel shows and thought, "I can do that . . ."

CHAPTER 1
Beginning in Oakland

Zendaya Maree Stoermer Coleman was born on September 1, 1996, in Oakland, California. The name *Zendaya* is inspired by the word *tendai*

from the Shona language, which is spoken in Zimbabwe. Tendai means "to give thanks." Her mother, Claire Stoermer, is from a German and Scottish background. Zendaya's father, Kazembe Ajamu, was born Samuel David Coleman, but he changed his name to reconnect to his family's African roots. When Zendaya was born, he already had five children from another marriage. Although her three brothers and two sisters are much older, they have always been an important part of Zendaya's life.

Both of Zendaya's parents were teachers. But they worked at two very different types of schools. Her father taught at a private school that Zendaya attended for elementary school. Many of the students were wealthy. And Zendaya noticed that she was one of the few Black students. But things were very different at the public school where her mother taught. Some students there were immigrants. Some were from struggling families.

Zendaya saw how different opportunities could be for kids who didn't even live that far away from each other. "I was lucky to go to a private school that provided computer science activities/courses," she told *Essence* magazine. "As a child, I could clearly see that the public school where my mom taught did not have the same resources, not even close."

Zendaya was a very shy, quiet child. She didn't speak at all in kindergarten. Her parents decided to have her repeat the grade. They hoped it would give her a chance to catch up socially with other children.

At first, it seemed like sports might be Zendaya's passion. Both of her parents had played basketball and they got Zendaya interested in it at an early age. She loved the game and was good at it, too.

But she already had her mind on something else. Like many kids, Zendaya enjoyed the shows on the Disney Channel. As she watched the young actors sing and dance, she found herself thinking she'd like to do the same thing. When she was six, she got her first chance to perform. She sang with her father at a school event. Her voice was strong and everyone was impressed.

Zendaya's mother had a summer job as a house manager for the California Shakespeare Theater. By the time Zendaya was seven, she was helping her mother out at the theater. She passed out programs to audience members and then stayed for the shows. Zendaya was enchanted by the theater world. She spent hours watching long rehearsals and never got bored.

Zendaya became interested in dancing, and joined a hip-hop dance troupe called Future Shock Oakland when she was in third grade. Her mother also signed her up for children's classes at the California Shakespeare Theater. She hoped that would help with Zendaya's shyness. The classes taught Zendaya the basics of acting. And

she got to perform scenes from Shakespeare's plays, like *Macbeth*, *As You Like It*, and *Richard III*.

Zendaya was becoming serious about acting. She began to get cast in plays at big local theaters. She worked with an acting coach to prepare for important auditions. Soon, her father was taking her on the long drive from Oakland to Los Angeles so she could try out for professional jobs.

Her first jobs were modeling for stores like Old Navy and Macy's and as a dancer in a Kidz Bop video. In one Sears commercial, she was a backup dancer for Disney star Selena Gomez.

People began to notice Zendaya. A casting director for the Disney Channel named Judy Taylor thought she stood out from other kids. "You never tire of watching her," Taylor said.

When Disney began to plan a new show about teen dancers in 2009, Taylor remembered Zendaya.

More than two hundred young actors auditioned for the lead roles in the show. Disney kept bringing Zendaya back to dance and act in more rounds of auditions.

Finally, they made a decision. Zendaya and Bella Thorne were cast as the leads in the show, *Shake It Up*. Zendaya was going to be a Disney Channel star, just as she had once imagined. She was thirteen years old and on her way.

CHAPTER 2
Shaking It Up

On *Shake It Up*, Zendaya played Raquel "Rocky" Blue, with Bella Thorne as her best friend, CeCe Jones. The two starred as Chicago teens who were cast as backup dancers on a show called *Shake It Up, Chicago*. Episodes focused on how they balanced their lives as professional dancers with their everyday lives at school. The show gave Zendaya plenty of chances to show off her dance skills, as well as her comic talent. Her screen credits listed her name as just Zendaya. She later told *Allure* magazine that she dropped her last name because "I just thought it was cool, like Cher or Prince."

Making *Shake It Up* was a lot of work, but it was fun. Zendaya and Bella spent a lot of time together both filming the show and taking classes on set. They became good friends in real life, just like on the show.

The hardest part was being away from home. Zendaya's father had moved with her to Los Angeles, where the show was filmed. But her mother stayed in Oakland so she could keep her teaching job. Zendaya was very close to her mom and really missed her— and her dog, Midnight, too.

Shake It Up premiered on November 7, 2010. It quickly became one of Disney's most popular shows.

Starring in *Shake It Up* led to more opportunities for Zendaya. In 2011, she released her first solo single, "Swag It Out." She and Bella starred in *Frenemies*, a Disney Channel movie, in 2012. They also sang together on several songs for the *Shake It Up* soundtracks.

Shake It Up ran for three seasons, ending in 2013. Zendaya attracted a lot of fans from her work on the show. Many of them felt like they grew up with her.

Zendaya took her fans seriously. She communicated with people through social media and tried to be a good role model. In 2013, she published an advice book for tweens, called *Between U and Me: How to Rock Your Tween Years with Style and Confidence*. In the book, she answered questions about life she'd received from her fans through social media. She offered advice about things like how to handle difficult situations at school, and how to be a good friend.

When *Shake It Up* ended, Zendaya had time to focus on music. She released another single, "Replay," in 2013, followed by her first full-length album. She performed songs from the album live at a number of music festivals over the next two years.

But that wasn't all Zendaya did in 2013. That year, she became the youngest person to compete on *Dancing with the Stars*! Although Zendaya had danced a lot, she didn't have much experience with the type of ballroom dancing that is a big part of the show. She had to learn a new routine every week and then perform it live for the show's judges. But she worked hard and came in second place.

Zendaya performed on the show as a way to learn more about herself. The experience was

both challenging and scary. She said her time on the show was a good way to break out and do something different. And it was the perfect opportunity to begin to show her talent to audiences beyond the Disney Channel. Zendaya wanted people to know that she could do more than viewers had seen on *Shake It Up*.

CHAPTER 3
Taking Charge

In 2013, Disney talked to Zendaya about two new upcoming projects. One was a movie for the Disney Channel called *Zapped.* The other was a new series, called *Super Awesome Katy.* In it, Zendaya would star as a girl named Katy who becomes a spy like her character's parents.

But Zendaya had other ideas. She was no longer the unknown little girl who had been cast in *Shake It Up.* She was now seventeen years old. And she had proven herself. She had some power and she wanted to use it for good.

Zendaya met with Disney executives. She asked to be named a producer on the show. A producer gets to make important decisions about a TV show or movie. Then she said she wanted to rename the show—and the character. "Do I look like a Katy to you?" she asked. She also didn't want the character to be another dancer or singer. Instead, Zendaya suggested that she play a girl who was trained in martial arts, was good at math, and was more awkward than popular. She wanted to show a different type of girl than the ones on other Disney shows.

Most importantly, she wanted the show to be about a family of color. Zendaya hadn't seen many families like hers on TV when she was growing up. She wanted to make sure that other Black kids had a chance to see a strong character who looked like them. They could be heroes, too.

Disney agreed with Zendaya's ideas. The show became *K.C. Undercover*. Zendaya played K.C., a smart teen who could fight and get out of tough situations. Her family was Black. And Zendaya was one of the show's producers. The first episode of *K.C. Undercover* ran on January 18, 2015.

As a young TV star, Zendaya had many chances to go to big events and awards shows. She had always loved fashion and getting dressed up. She thought it was a way to express herself and try on different looks and characters. She still thought of herself as shy, but when she put on an exciting outfit for a photo shoot, she felt bold and confident.

Back in 2011, Zendaya had met a fashion stylist named Law Roach. She liked his ideas and felt he understood what she wanted. They kept working together, and Zendaya became known for her fantastic style on the red carpet and in photo shoots.

In February 2015, Zendaya was invited to the Academy Awards ceremony. It was the biggest movie night of the year. It also was one of the biggest fashion events of the year. Viewers liked to watch stars walk the red carpet in their glamorous outfits.

For the event, Zendaya wore a beautiful white gown made by a famous designer. Her hair was styled in locs. Most people thought she looked amazing. But the next day, a fashion reporter on TV made a mean, racist joke about her hairstyle.

Zendaya was angry and hurt. She understood that hair is a sensitive issue for Black women. She remembered how when she was in grammar school, the only time someone complimented her hair was when she straightened it. Now, she thought carefully about what she wanted to say. The next day she posted her reply on social media.

Zendaya wrote about all the people she knew and loved who wore locs, including members of her family, and other talented, accomplished Black people. She stated, "My wearing my hair in locs on an Oscar red carpet was to showcase them in a positive light, to remind people of color that our hair is good enough. To me locs are a symbol of strength and beauty, almost like a lion's mane."

People applauded Zendaya's strong, thoughtful response. The reporter apologized to her. The toy company Mattel decided to make a Barbie doll version of Zendaya in her Oscar dress—and locs!

Years later, Zendaya talked about that Oscars moment. She said it made her think, "How could I always have a lasting impact on what people saw and associated with people of color?"

CHAPTER 4
Making Movies

In 2015, Zendaya graduated from Oak Park Independent School, a private school that allowed her to do her schoolwork while continuing her career. She was still starring in *K.C. Undercover*, but she was also keeping busy with other projects, like guest-starring on an episode of the ABC sitcom *black-ish*. She played the character Cut-Throat in Taylor Swift's video for "Bad Blood." In 2016, she was in Beyoncé's video for the song "All Night." That video was part of Beyoncé's visual album *Lemonade*, and Zendaya felt honored to be included with other young Black stars like Amandla Stenberg and Chloe x Halle. On her Instagram, she posted a photo from the video shoot and wrote, "One of the most beautiful things I've ever had the honor of being a part of . . . Black. Girl. Magic." In 2016, she became the face of Cover Girl cosmetics, appearing in print and TV ads for the brand.

Also in 2016, Zendaya was asked to audition for a Marvel movie. The Marvel franchise is famous for its big superhero movies, like the Avengers series and *Captain America*. Zendaya wasn't supposed to know *which* movie she was trying out for. But her agents found out that it would be a new Spider-Man movie. She didn't know much about the role, though. She thought it was just a small part.

The director, Jon Watts, didn't recognize her on the audition tape. She wore no makeup and seemed very different than the Zendaya he thought he knew from the Disney Channel. Watts loved Zendaya's audition, and in March 2016, Marvel announced that she had been cast in *Spider-Man: Homecoming*. She would play Michelle, also known as MJ. Her character was friends with Peter Parker (Spider-Man), to be played by Tom Holland. Robert Downey Jr. would again appear as Tony Stark/Iron Man, one of the Avengers.

Before her work on *Homecoming* began, Zendaya auditioned for another film. *The Greatest Showman* would star Hugh Jackman as P. T. Barnum, the nineteenth-century circus owner. Zendaya impressed the director, Michael Gracey, and one of the other stars, Zac Efron, by making her own recording of "Rewrite the Stars," one of the songs written for the movie. She was cast in the part of Anne Wheeler, a young trapeze artist.

Zendaya filmed *Homecoming* throughout the summer of 2016. Most of the cast members were close to her age, and they quickly became good friends. But as soon as she finished *Homecoming*,

Zendaya had to rush off to begin rehearsals for *The Greatest Showman*. And she had to learn how to fly on the trapeze! Of course she would have stunt doubles for the most difficult parts. But the director wanted to be able to use Zendaya for the action as much as possible. It was difficult work. But it also was fun.

The next year was huge for the young star. In June 2017, *Spider-Man: Homecoming* was released. It became one of the biggest hits of the year. People especially liked Zendaya's comic performance as the sarcastic Michelle.

At the end of 2017, *The Greatest Showman* also was released. It stayed in movie theaters for months and became one of the highest-earning live-action musical films ever. Zendaya's duet with Zac Efron, "Rewrite the Stars," also became a hit.

In 2018, Zendaya heard about a new show being planned by HBO called *Euphoria*. It was based on an Israeli TV drama about high-school students dealing with mental health issues, drugs, and death. Sam Levinson, a writer and director, was in charge of the US version. It focused on a high-school girl named Rue, who was struggling with drug addiction and depression. Levinson based most of the story on his own experiences.

Zendaya's managers weren't sure it was the right kind of role for her. It was so different from the other characters she had played. But Zendaya loved the script. She wanted to be challenged as an actor. After filming *Spider-Man: Far from Home* during the summer of 2018, Zendaya went to work on *Euphoria*.

CHAPTER 5
Euphoria

The first season of *Euphoria* filmed from October 2018 through May 2019. After that, Zendaya was cast in *Dune*, an epic science fiction movie based on the well-known book by Frank Herbert. Zendaya was set to play Chani, a mysterious young woman who lives on a desert planet.

Chani was a small part in the first movie, but a sequel was already planned where she would play a much bigger role. And filming was exciting. Zendaya thought it was cool to get a chance to dress up like the warrior character in the setting of giant rocks in the desert. She also threw dance parties for the cast in her dressing room when they weren't filming.

When *Euphoria* premiered on HBO in June 2019, people were stunned by Zendaya's performance. They had known her as a young

singer and dancer. They had seen her as Spider-Man's funny friend, and as a glamorous fashion star. But as Rue in *Euphoria*, she proved that she

could play deeply emotional, dramatic characters. Zendaya was now taken seriously as one of Hollywood's top young actors.

Zendaya was already set to film her third Spider-Man movie and the *Dune* sequel. She represented several cosmetic brands and had created her own fashion collection with designer Tommy Hilfiger. Other famous designers were anxious to have her wear their clothes on photo shoots. And she was getting ready to film another season of *Euphoria*.

Then, in March 2020, the COVID-19 pandemic shut down all her work plans.

Like many others, Zendaya had to quarantine at home. She tried different things to keep busy, like hiking with her dog, Noon, and painting. Like many Americans, Zendaya was deeply hurt by the incidents of violence against Black people that unfolded during 2020 and spoke out in support of protesters marching for racial justice.

But Zendaya had been working almost nonstop since she was thirteen years old. Acting was a big part of her life. She missed having the chance to create and portray new characters. While talking to *Euphoria* creator Sam Levinson, she wondered whether it would be possible to make a small movie during quarantine. Levinson came up with a script called *Malcolm & Marie*. It was written for just two actors and could be filmed in a single location with a small crew.

Zendaya starred along with John David Washington. Levinson directed. Everyone quarantined together at the house where they filmed. They shot the black-and-white film in only two weeks. Zendaya was proud of her work in *Malcolm & Marie*. It also was her first movie credit as a producer.

Late in 2020, Zendaya was able to reunite with her Spider-Man friends to film *Spider-Man:*

No Way Home. After that, she began filming season two of *Euphoria.*

Dune had been held back from movie theaters due to the pandemic. But it finally premiered in September 2021 at the Venice International Film Festival. At the festival, Zendaya walked the red carpet in a leather gown and an emerald and diamond necklace. *Dune* was released in theaters and online in October 2021.

Spider-Man: No Way Home was released on December 17, 2021. At the film's premiere, Zendaya wore a brown Valentino gown that featured a spiderweb design made from black crystals. *No Way Home* became the highest-earning movie of 2021 and the sixth highest-earning movie of all time.

Season two of *Euphoria* premiered in January 2022. For the red carpet at the premiere, Zendaya wore a black-and-white-striped gown from the designer Valentino's 1992 collection. Again, viewers were impressed by Zendaya's realistic performance as troubled teen Rue. In February, HBO announced that there would be a third season of the show.

Zendaya often describes herself as a perfectionist. In *Interview* magazine she said, "I'm always afraid to do things in fear of not being great. But the only way to get great is to be fearless and try."

She still thinks of herself as a quiet person who would rather stay home with her dog than go to Hollywood parties. But she also knows she can use her voice and her platform to help others. Zendaya hopes that watching *Euphoria* will help people understand those who suffer from addiction. She has thought about being a director. She wants to tell more stories that focus on Black people and wants to make sure that Hollywood gives more chances to people of color.

Giving Back

Throughout her career, Zendaya has used her success to help others, most especially on her own birthday. She donated book bags stuffed with school supplies to children in Oakland for

her fifteenth and sixteenth birthdays. On her eighteenth birthday, she worked with feedONE to raise money to feed at least 150 children in Haiti, Tanzania, and the Philippines. For her twentieth birthday, in 2016, she worked to raise $50,000 for Convoy of Hope's Women's Empowerment Initiative.

In her 2020 Emmy Award acceptance speech, Zendaya said she saw hope in young people. But she is also one of the dynamic and talented young people who hopes to help the world change.

Timeline of Zendaya's Life

1996 — Zendaya Maree Stoermer Coleman is born on September 1 in Oakland, California

2004 — Joins hip-hop troupe Future Shock Oakland

2010 — Stars as Raquel "Rocky" Blue in Disney Channel show *Shake It Up*

2011 — Releases single "Swag It Out"

2012 — Stars in Disney Channel movie *Frenemies*

2013 — Appears on *Dancing with the Stars*

— Releases album *Zendaya* in September

2014 — Stars in Disney Channel movie *Zapped*

2015 — Stars in and produces Disney Channel show *K.C. Undercover*

— Graduates from Oak Park Independent School

2017 — Plays Michelle "MJ" Jones-Watson in *Spider-Man: Homecoming*

— Plays Anne Wheeler in *The Greatest Showman*

2019 — Stars as Rue in HBO show *Euphoria* and as MJ in *Spider-Man: Far from Home*

2020 — Wins Emmy for Outstanding Lead Actress in a Drama Series

2021 — Plays Chani in *Dune*

— Stars in *Spider-Man: No Way Home*

Timeline of the World

1996 — The Spice Girls release their first album, *Spice*, in the UK and Japan

1999 — *SpongeBob SquarePants* premieres

2001 — Terrorist attacks on 9/11 kill 2,996 people in New York, Pennsylvania, and Washington, DC

2004 — The Nintendo DS is released

2006 — The Twitter app is launched

2007 — The Great Recession begins in the United States in December

2011 — The full version of the video game *Minecraft* is released

2013 — Terrorist bombs at the Boston Marathon kill 3 people and injure 264

2016 — Britain votes to leave the European Union in a move known as Brexit

2017 — Hurricane Harvey devastates parts of Texas and Louisiana

2019 — Scientists capture the first images of a black hole in space

2020 — The COVID-19 pandemic begins

2021 — At age ninety, actor William Shatner becomes the oldest person to fly into space

2022 — Russia invades Ukraine

Bibliography

"Actually Me: Zendaya Responds to Fans on the Internet." *GQ*.
February 2021. YouTube video, 11:12. https://www.youtube.
com/watch?v=buMCmzXJUxo.

Aguirre, Abby. "Zendaya Talks *Spider-Man*, Her First Love, and
Reinventing Disney Stardom." *Vogue*. June 15, 2017. https://
www.vogue.com/article/zendaya-interview-july-vogue-
cover-spider-man-homecoming.

Chalamet, Timothée. "Bow Down, It's Zendaya." *Elle UK*.
October 11, 2020. https://www.elle.com/uk/life-and-culture/
culture/a34617948/zendaya-december-cover-interview/.

Cullors, Patrisse. "Zendaya on Where We Go from Here." *InStyle*.
August 6, 2020. https://www.instyle.com/celebrity/zendaya-
september-2020-cover.

Domingo, Colman. "Zendaya Tells Colman Domingo How She
Found New Purpose." *Interview*. December 7, 2021. https://
www.interviewmagazine.com/culture/zendaya-tells-colman-
domingo-how-she-found-purpose.

Jackson, Dory. "Zendaya Admits to Feeling a 'Heavy Responsibility'
to Represent Black Women in Hollywood." *Us Weekly*. June 25,
2020. https://www.usmagazine.com/celebrity-news/news/
zendaya-feels-a-heavy-responsibility-to-represent-black-
women/.

Janiak, Lily. "Zendaya Was a Shy, Quiet Child. Bay Area Theater Showed Her a Path to 'Euphoria.'" *San Francisco Chronicle Datebook*. November 4, 2020. https://datebook. sfchronicle.com/theater/zendaya-was-a-shy-quiet-child-bay-area-theater-showed-her-a-path-to-euphoria.

Meltzer, Marisa. "'There's So Much I Want to Do': The World According to Zendaya." *British Vogue*. September 6, 2021. https://www.vogue.co.uk/news/article/zendaya-british-vogue-interview.

Mendoza, Paola, director. "Z for Zendaya." I Am an Immigrant. June 9, 2015. YouTube video, 3:49. https://www.youtube.com/watch?v=ZAERsh8e7IU.

Peone, Vince, director. "73 Questions with Zendaya." *Vogue*. May 31, 2019. YouTube video, 12:12. https://www.youtube.com/watch?v=MGO4_8YRKr0.

Sandell, Laurie. "Zendaya Explains the Real Reason She Came Back to Disney." *Cosmopolitan*. June 2, 2016. https://www.cosmopolitan.com/entertainment/news/a59215/zendaya-july-2016/.

Siegel, Elizabeth. "Zendaya Opens Up About Her Buzzy 'Spider-Man' Role, Cultural Appropriation, and Her Future with Disney." *Allure*. December 13, 2016. https://www.allure.com/story/zendaya-disney-cultural-appropriation-interview.

Williams, Kam. "Zendaya: Shaking It Up." *Bay State
    Banner*. August 31, 2011. https://www.baystatebanner.
    com/2011/08/31/the-young-actress-talks-about-her-hit-
    sitcom-and-living-her-childhood-dreams/.

YOUR HEADQUARTERS FOR HISTORY

Activities, Mad Libs, and sidesplitting jokes!
Discover the Who HQ books beyond the biographies

Who? What? Where?

Learn more at whohq.com!